Contents

KT-116-205

Any words appearing in the text in bold, **like this**, are explained in the Glossary.

Introducing sponges and other minor phyla

Sponges, cnidarians, worms and echinoderms are all **invertebrates**. They are animals that do not have a backbone. These groups of animals are found around the world. Earthworms live in soil, while sponges, cnidarians (jellyfish and corals) and echinoderms (starfish and sea urchins) are found in coral **reefs** and shallow coastal waters.

Animals without backbones

Animals such as mammals, birds and fish have a backbone that supports their body. Invertebrates do not have a backbone, so they need some other form of support. The starfish gets its support from spiny plates that lie just beneath the skin. Many invertebrates, for example the earthworm, have a hydroskeleton. This means that their **skeleton** is formed from a fluid-filled body space. The fluid pushes against their body wall and makes it fairly rigid. A few invertebrates, for example jellyfish, have no skeleton at all. They are supported by the water in which they live.

▼ These **anemones** belong to the phylum Cnidaria. Their simple bodies do not have any skeletons.

Classification key

KINGDOM	Animalia
PHYLA	**Porifera, Cnidaria, Plathelminthes, Nematoda, Annelida, Echinodermata**
SPECIES	20,000 (total for all these phyla)

Sponges
and other minor phyla

Sally Morgan

www.raintreepublishers.co.uk
Visit our website to find out more information about **Raintree** books.

To order:
☎ Phone 44 (0) 1865 888113
🗎 Send a fax to 44 (0) 1865 314091
💻 Visit the Raintree Bookshop at **www.raintreepublishers.co.uk** to browse our catalogue and order online.

Produced for Raintree by
White-Thomson Publishing Ltd
Bridgewater Business Centre, 210 High Street,
Lewes, East Sussex, BN7 2NH

First published in Great Britain by Raintree,
Halley Court, Jordan Hill, Oxford, OX2 8EJ,
part of Harcourt Education.
Raintree is a registered trademark of Harcourt Education Ltd.

Consultant: Dr Rod Preston-Mafham
Editorial: Alison Cooper, Nick Hunter and Catherine Clarke
Design: Tim Mayer
Picture Research: Morgan Interactive Ltd
Production: Amanda Meaden

Originated by Dot Gradations Ltd
Printed in China by WKT Company Limited

ISBN 1 844 43774 4 (hardback)   ISBN 1 844 43784 1 (paperback)
09 08 07 06 05   10 09 08 07 06
10 9 8 7 6 5 4 3 2 1   10 9 8 7 6 5 4 3 2 1

British Library Cataloguing in Publication Data
Morgan, Sally
Sponges and Other Minor Phyla. – (Animal Kingdom)
593
A full catalogue record for this book is available from the British Library.

Acknowledgements
The publishers would like to thank the following for permission to reproduce photographs: Adds, John p. **30**; Corbis pp. **6**, **61**; Digital Vision p. **57** bottom; Ecoscene **contents** main image (John Liddiard), **contents** left and right (Jeff Collett), **4** (Phillip Colla), **5** left (John Liddiard), **8** (Jeff Collett), **9** top (John Liddiard), **9** bottom (Phillip Colla), **11** bottom (Jeff Collett), **12** left, **13** (John Liddiard), **15** (Phillip Colla), **21** main (John Liddiard), **23** bottom (Phillip Colla), **26** (Kjell Sandved), **29** bottom (John Lewis), **34** top (Wayne Lawler), **34** bottom (Kjell Sandved), **35** (Mark Caney), **37** top (Kjell Sandved), **37** bottom (Mark Caney), **39** right (Jeff Collett), **44** bottom (Phillip Colla), **46**, **47** (John Liddiard), **48** (Jeff Collett), **49** bottom (John Liddiard), **51** top (Kjell Sandved), **54** (John Liddiard), **55** top (Mark Caney), **55** bottom (Martha Collard), **56** (John Liddiard), **57** top (Wayne Lawler), **60** top (Frank Blackburn), **60** bottom (Jeff Collett); Ecoscene-Papilio pp. **18** main (Steve Jones), **28**, **31** top, **33**, **38-39**, **40**, **41** top (Robert Pickett), **52** top (Peter Tatton), Mediscan p **31** bottom; Nature Photo Library pp. **7** top (Jeff Rotman), **21** inset (David Shale), **27** bottom (Sinclair Stammers), **36** (Constantinos Petrinos); NHPA pp. **5** right (Trevor McDonald), **11** top (G Bernard), **12-13** (Image Quest 3-D), **14** top (M Walker), **14** bottom (Image Quest 3-D), **17** top (Michael Patrick O'Neill), **17** bottom (Norbert Wu), **20** (Rich Kirchner), **22** (Peter Parks), **23** top (Anthony Bannister), **24** (ANT), **25** (Image Quest 3-D), **27** top, **29** top (M Walker), **32** top (Image Quest 3-D), **38** left (B Jones and M Shimlock), **41** bottom (Nigel Callow), **42** top (Stephen Dalton), **42** bottom (Martin Harvey), **43** (Anthony Bannister), **45** (Trevor McDonald), **49** top (Pete Atkinson), **50** (Trevor McDonald), **51** bottom (G Bernard), **52** bottom, **53** (B Jones and M Shimlock); Photodisc **title**, pp. **10**, **16**, **19**, **44** top, **57** bottom, **58**, **59**, **62**, **63**, **64**; Premaphoto Wildlife pp. **7** bottom (Cliff Nelson), **32** bottom (Preston Mafham).

Front cover image of sponges colonizing a wreck is reproduced with permission of Ecoscene (V & W); back cover image of a starfish is reproduced with permission of Digital Vision.

Every effort has been made to contact copyright holders of any material reproduced in this book. Any omissions will be rectified in subsequent printings if notice is given to the publishers.

The paper used to print this book comes from sustainable resources.

Sponges, jellyfish and many other invertebrates live their entire lives in water. Most live in salt water, but a few are found in the fresh water of ponds, lakes and rivers. Some invertebrates, such as the earthworm, live on land. Most invertebrates can move around, but a surprising number cannot. They stay in the same place all the time and are called **sessile**. Others are described as being **sedentary** because they move very little.

The groups of animals that are featured in this book are sponges, cnidarians, flatworms, roundworms, segmented worms and echinoderms.

▲ There are many different types of worm. These peacock worms are segmented worms belonging to the phylum Annelida.

▲ Starfish are spiny-skinned invertebrates that belong to the phylum Echinodermata. They are closely related to sea urchins and brittlestars.

Classification

Living **organisms** are classified, or organized, according to how closely related one organism is to another. A **species** is a group of individuals that are similar to each other and that can **interbreed** with one another, for example humans belong to the species *Homo sapiens*. Species are grouped together into genera (singular: genus). A genus may contain a number of species that share some features. Genera are grouped together in families, the families grouped into orders and the orders grouped into classes. Classes are grouped together in phyla (singular: phylum) and finally the phyla are grouped into kingdoms. Kingdoms are the largest groups. Sponges and all the other invertebrate animals belong to the animal kingdom.

Sponges

A sponge is the simplest of animals. Its body does not have any organs or nerves. It is just a collection of cells held together by a network of fibres. Sponges do not move from one place to another. They are **sessile** animals that stay attached to the same place. Most attach themselves to any suitable surface such as rocks, seaweed or even other animals. A few bore into rocks, shells or coral.

Most sponges are marine. They are found in all the seas, mainly in shallow water, although a few are found in deep water. They even occur in great numbers in the cold waters around Antarctica, where they can grow to large sizes. A few sponges live in fresh water.

Classification key

PHYLUM	**Porifera**
CLASSES	4 (Calcarea, Demospongiae, Hexactinellida, Sclerospongiae)
ORDERS	18
SPECIES	10,000

◄ Sponges come in an incredible variety of colours and shapes. These are tube sponges, which are open at one end and closed at the other. Other shapes include spheres, branching and thread-like sponges.

Skeleton and shape

The **skeleton** of the sponge has two main parts. There are fibres of collagen called spongin and rods with many points called **spicules**. Spicules may be made from silica or calcium carbonate. As well as providing support, the spicules provide protection from **predators**. Few predators try to eat a sponge – it would be like trying to swallow a mouthful of splinters.

Since sponges do not have a **nervous system**, they hardly react to the environment around them. The only reaction they show is slowly to change the size of the opening (**osculum**) through which water leaves their body. This is triggered by changes in the water around them, for example by a change in the temperature or current. Sponges also lack co-ordination between cells for growth and, as a result, they are of irregular size and shape. Often individual sponges are part of a larger mass, or **colony**, and it is almost impossible to identify the individuals, other than by the osculum.

Protected by poisons

Sponges have few predators. Over millions of years, they have developed an array of poisons to keep away animals that might eat them and plants that might grow over them. These chemicals are so effective that research is underway to identify them for use in medicines.

▲ Some sponges grow to a great size. The osculum of this sponge is large enough for a diver to swim inside.

Amazing facts

- A living bath sponge looks more like a piece of raw liver than the sponges we are used to using. The sponges are killed by boiling, leaving the skeleton behind. This is cleaned and trimmed for use by humans.

- Millions of years ago, some of the first **reefs** made by animals were made of sponges. The corals later outperformed them as reef-forming animals.

▲ The azure vase sponge is one of the most attractive sponges with its beautiful light blue to purple colour.

Feeding and life cycle

Sponges do not have a mouth. Instead, they have tiny pores in their outer walls through which water is drawn. Cells in the wall filter particles of food from the water. The water enters a central cavity and is then expelled through a large opening called the **osculum**. The water flows in one direction and is driven by the beating of **flagella** (long, hair-like structures), which line the surface of the cavity.

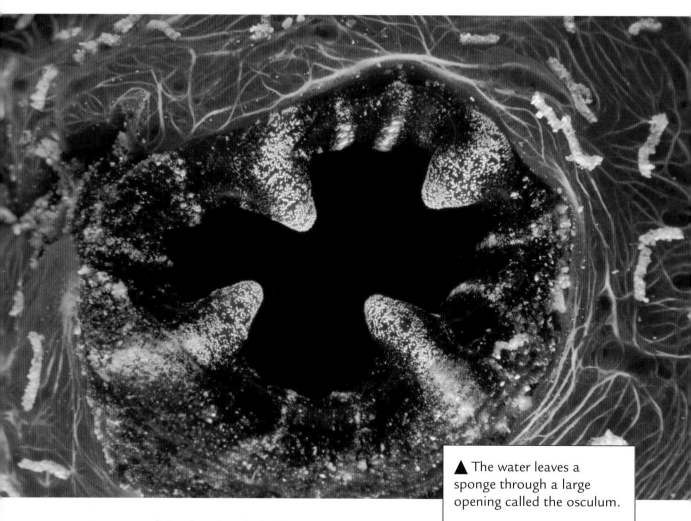

▲ The water leaves a sponge through a large opening called the osculum.

Sponges of the family Cladorhizidae are unusual in that they are **carnivores**. They feed by capturing and digesting animals such as small **crustaceans**. When the sponge comes into contact with its **prey**, its **spicules** stick to the prey so it cannot escape. The sponge's cells move around the prey and pour digestive juices over its body. Slowly the body of the prey is broken down. Then the sponge cells absorb the nutrients.

Scientists are unsure why sponges come in so many colours. The vivid colours may be a warning that the sponge is poisonous or distasteful, or they may be a form of protection from the harmful rays of the sun.

Life cycle

Sponges reproduce by both asexual and sexual means. **Asexual reproduction** only involves one parent and all the offspring are identical to the parent. Sponges that reproduce asexually produce buds. A bud consists of a collection of cells of various kinds inside a protective covering. The bud is released and it settles on the seabed and grows into a new sponge. All the new sponges are identical to the parent sponge that produced the bud.

Most sponges that undergo **sexual reproduction** are **hermaphrodite**. This means each sponge produces both eggs and sperm, but at different times of year. The sponges release their sperm into the water and they are carried on currents to other sponges where the sperm **fertilize** the eggs. A fertilized egg develops into a ciliated **larva**. This is a larva covered in tiny hairs called **cilia**. These larvae swim in the water and then settle on the seabed and develop into young sponges.

Amazing facts

- Some of the smaller **species** of Demospongiae bore into mollusc shells, leaving the shell riddled with tiny holes.
- If a sponge is forced though a sieve, so that it is separated into individual cells, these cells will eventually reorganize themselves back into a sponge.
- Sometimes young prawns enter sponges and live inside them, becoming too large to get out again.

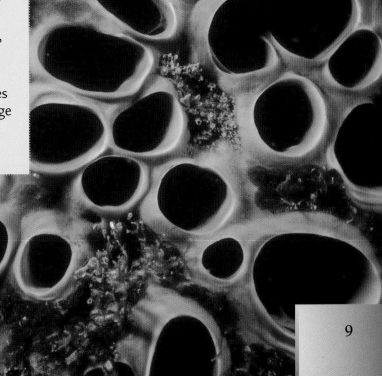

► This close-up view of the grey moon sponge shows a number of oscula on the upper surface of the sponge.

9

Sponge classification

▲ The vase shape of this sponge does not help in its identification. Cells must be collected and examined under a microscope in order to identify the species.

Sponges belong to the phylum Porifera. A single **species** of sponge may occur in different shapes, so identification often depends on the type and shape of the **spicules**, which are unique to each species. In the past, the classification of sponges was based just on the type of spicules. This created four classes of sponge: Calcarea, Demospongiae, Hexactinellida and Sclerospongiae. However, recent evidence taken from **fossil** sponges suggests that the Sclerospongiae are not sufficiently different to be classified separately from the other classes.

Calcarea

Calcarea sponges are the only class of sponge to have spicules made of calcium carbonate. The spicules have one, three or four rays or points. There are approximately 100 species, most of which are small sponges, found in shallow water, as well as in caves and on seaweed.

Demospongiae

This is the largest class with 9500 species and it includes the best-known group of sponges, the bath sponges. These sponges are found in both shallow and deep water, nearly always on a solid surface. Demospongiae have spicules made from silica with one, two or four rays. The sponges can reach up to 1 metre in length or width and are often brightly coloured.

Amazing facts

- So many sponges of the class Demospongiae are collected for use as bath sponges that some species are threatened with **extinction**.
- Some sponges found in fresh water are bright green. The colour comes from single-celled algae living in their cells.

Hexactinellida

The Hexactinellida, or 'glass sponges', have spicules made from silica with six rays. There are about 500 species living in cold water at depths of between 200 and 2000 metres. One beautiful example is a sponge called Venus' Flower Basket. It has an intricate 3-D **skeleton**, which is only structurally possible because of the variety of ways in which the six-rayed spicules fit together.

▲ The Venus' flower basket is named after its beautiful lacework of silica spicules. It is found in deep water off the Philippines.

Sclerospongiae

The coralline sponges, or Sclerospongiae, are an unusual class in which the sponges have a skeleton of silica and calcium carbonate. There is a thin living layer containing spicules of silica, which covers a massive solid skeleton made of calcium carbonate. A few living species are found on coral **reefs** around the West Indies and in the Pacific Ocean.
The remaining species only exist as fossils.

Classification key

PHYLUM	Porifera
CLASSES	4 (Calcarea, Demospongiae, Hexactinellida, Sclerospongiae)
FAMILIES	80
SPECIES	10,000

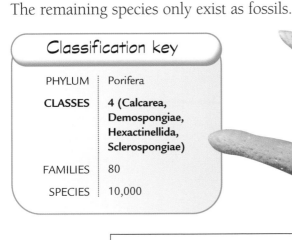

▶ Sponges come in a great range of shapes. One of the most unusual is this hand-shaped sponge.

Cnidaria

Sea **anemones**, corals and jellyfish are all examples of cnidarians. These are sac-shaped animals with **tentacles** covered in sting cells.

Body shapes

Cnidarians do not have a proper head. They have a single body opening that is called the mouth. The body is sac-like and encloses a large central cavity called the enteron, which connects to the outside through the mouth. The enteron is used for digestion and for gas exchange, in which oxygen is taken in and carbon dioxide is given out. The mouth is surrounded by tentacles, which are studded with microscopic sting cells. Most cnidarians are **radially symmetrical** – they have many lines of symmetry around a central point.

▶ Jellyfish have a bell-shaped body and many long tentacles that hang in the water below their bell.

Classification key

PHYLUM	Cnidaria
CLASSES	Anthozoa, Scyphozoa, Hydrozoa, Cubozoa
ORDERS	7
SPECIES	approximately 9000

▼ Soft corals are brightly coloured and belong to the class Anthozoa.

The tentacles are arranged in a circle around the mouth and are covered in microscopic sting cells.

The body of a cnidarian has two cell layers.

The slimy disc at the bottom allows the anemone to slide about very slowly, but also to grip the rocks firmly.

▲ This dahlia anemone belongs to the class Anthozoa. Anemones grip the rocks so firmly that it is almost impossible to pull a sea anemone from its rock.

Two cell layers

Cnidarians are described as being **diploblastic**. This means that their body and tentacles consist of two cell layers: an inner layer called the endoderm and an outer layer called the ectoderm. Between the two cell layers is the mesogloea, which joins them both together.

Feeding

All cnidarians are **carnivorous**. They use their tentacles and sting cells to capture their **prey**. There are several different forms of sting cell. One type releases a thread that ends in a poisonous barb. The thread shoots out with such force that the barb pierces the body of the prey and it then releases a poison that paralyses the animal. The other types of sting cell release threads that hold the prey. Some stick to the prey while others wrap themselves around it. The sting cells are only used once and then have to be replaced.

Amazing facts

- The tiny box jellyfish is the size of a peanut and is probably the most poisonous animal on Earth. It is found in warm oceans around the world and is known to have killed people swimming in the water.
- Cnidarians can distinguish between food and inedible objects. If a piece of paper were to land on a sea anemone it would not trigger the sting cells.
- The thick layer of mesogloea in a jellyfish protects it from the buffeting of the sea.

Life cycle

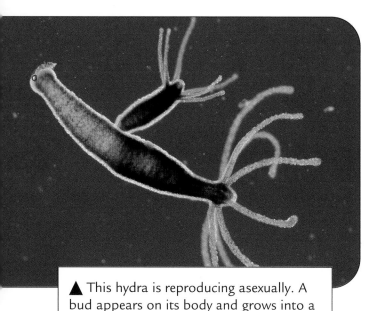

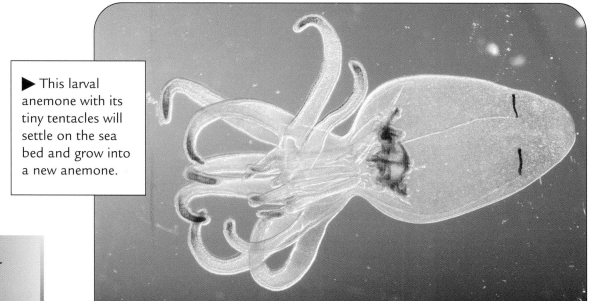

Cnidarians have a complex life cycle. They exist in two forms, the **polyp** and the **medusa**. The polyp is the **sedentary** form found on the seabed or on a coral **reef**. A typical polyp is a sea **anemone**, which has a ring of **tentacles** around its mouth. The medusa looks completely different from the polyp. It has a bell-shaped body like a jellyfish. Most cnidarians exist as a polyp for part of their life and as a medusa for the rest. They alternate between polyp and medusa. However there are some cnidarians, such as sea anemones and corals, which exist only as polyps.

▲ This hydra is reproducing asexually. A bud appears on its body and grows into a new individual. Eventually this new hydra will break away and become independent.

Polyp and medusa

The life cycle begins with the polyp. The polyp **reproduces** asexually to produce more identical polyps. This usually happens by budding – a bulge appears on the body wall of the polyp and develops into a new polyp. In some **species**, the bud grows, breaks off and develops into a new individual. In others, the new individual remains attached. As more individuals form, a **colony** develops with all the members of the colony connected by living tissue.

▶ This larval anemone with its tiny tentacles will settle on the sea bed and grow into a new anemone.

Amazing facts

- The word 'polyp' came from the French word *pouple*, which means 'octopus', because an early French naturalist thought the tentacles of a cnidarian resembled the tentacles of the octopus.
- The medusa is named after the unlucky woman in a Greek myth who was loved by the god of the sea. A jealous goddess turned her hair into snakes. The many tentacles on a cnidarian medusa reminded naturalists of Medusa's hair.

When conditions are right – for example, at a particular time of year or when the water reaches the right temperature – the polyp produces a medusa, which swims away. The medusa is the stage that undergoes **sexual reproduction**. It produces eggs and sperm, which are released into the sea. The sperm **fertilize** the eggs. Each fertilized egg develops into a **larva**, a pear-shaped animal covered in **cilia**. Then the larva undergoes a change in form, or metamorphosis. It settles on the seabed or rock, becomes attached and grows into a polyp. The life cycle begins again.

Members of the class Anthozoa, such as sea anemones, are different as they do not have a medusa stage. Some of their polyps can reproduce sexually by producing **gametes** (sex cells) instead. However, anthozoans rely on **asexual reproduction** to increase their numbers.

▶ Many tiny anemones can be seen under the tentacles of this adult anemone.

The flower animals

The class Anthozoa are often called the flower animals because of their bright colours and the way their **tentacles** form a ring like petals. They are marine animals and include corals, which build great **reefs** in **tropical** waters, as well as sea **anemones**, sea fans and sea pens. They are an ancient group of animals, dating back at least 550 million years. Anthozoans are found in the **intertidal zone** along the coasts, in the shallow warm waters around tropical islands and even in the deep ocean trenches more than 6 kilometres (3.7 miles) deep.

Anthozoan features

An anthozoan **polyp** has a cup-shaped body, with a mouth surrounded by a ring of hollow tentacles. Anthozoa range in size from tiny **species** just millimetres across to corals more than 10 metres across. They have sting cells to catch **prey**, just like other cnidarians. Sea anemones can feed on surprisingly large prey, such as fish and crabs. The smaller anthozoans, such as corals, have algae in their cells to provide them with food. They use their sting cells as protection against **predators** such as snails, starfish and sea spiders.

◀ Some anemones, such as these strawberry anemones, are found grouped together, whereas other species of anemone are solitary animals.

▲ A sea pen looks a bit like a feather. It has a central polyp with many lateral polyps arranged as side branches.

Reproduction

Anemones **reproduce** asexually by simply pulling apart into two halves. They can also reproduce sexually by producing **gametes** – eggs and sperm – which are released into the water. The resulting **larvae** settle on rocks and grow into new anemones.

Anthozoan classes

The Anthozoa is divided into three sub-classes. The Zoantharia includes the hard corals and most sea anemones. The Octocorallia includes the sea pens, soft corals and sea fans. The third sub-class, the Ceriantipatharia, includes the burrowing sea anemones and black corals.

▲ These sea anemones are fighting for position on the seabed, using their sting cells as weapons.

Amazing facts

- Some sea anemones live on the shells of snails and crabs. They are carried around by their **host**. They may get leftover food scraps from their host, and their host is protected from predators by the sea anemone's stinging tentacles.

- Sea anemones fight over **territory**, using their stings against other anemones. They keep stinging until the other anemone moves away. Sometimes these fights result in the anemones being injured or killed.

- The sea slug Aeolidia is one of the few animals that actually eats sea anemones. Its gut is lined with a protective coat to prevent injury from unexploded sting cells.

Classification key

PHYLUM	Cnidaria
CLASS	**Anthozoa**
SUB-CLASSES	Zoantharia, Octocorallia, Ceriantipatharia
SPECIES	more than 6500

Corals

Running down the length of the east coast of Australia is the Great Barrier **Reef**, a huge coral reef that can even be seen from space. Amazingly, it was built by tiny animals called corals over thousands of years. Corals are cnidarians that are related to sea **anemones**.

Classification key

PHYLUM	Cnidaria
CLASS	Anthozoa
SUB-CLASS	**Zoantharia, Octocorallia**
SPECIES	approximately 1000

▶ At first sight a coral reef looks like a garden, but corals are not plants. Corals are colonies of thousands of tiny animals that build upon one another.

Hard and soft corals

There are two types of warm-water corals: hard, or stony, corals and soft corals. It is the hard corals that are responsible for building the coral reefs. The hard corals live in **colonies** of individual **polyps** that share a common **skeleton**. The body of the polyp occupies a little cup, which is attached at the bottom. The polyp secretes a skeleton made of calcium carbonate (limestone). When the polyps die, they leave behind their skeleton. New polyps grow on top of the old, so over time the colony gets larger. The construction of a reef takes thousands, sometimes millions, of years.

▲ Soft corals have a flexible skeleton made of a protein called gorgonin. Their skeleton also contains calcium carbonate, but only in clumps of **spicules**.

Feeding

Corals use their **tentacles** to capture zooplankton, the small animals that live in the water. Most corals only extend their polyps and tentacles at night when zooplankton is most abundant, but the soft corals keep their polyps open throughout the day. The reef-building corals also get food from the algae that live in their cells, the **zooxanthellae**. The zooxanthellae carry out **photosynthesis**, using light and carbon dioxide to make carbohydrates, some of which are given to the coral animal. The reef-building corals can only live in warm, shallow water, down to depths of about 100 metres, because their algae need light to photosynthesize. This extra supply of food allows them to grow quickly and build new skeleton, which forms the reef. The zooxanthellae also give the corals their colour.

Reproduction

Coral polyps can **reproduce** asexually by dividing into two. They also reproduce sexually by releasing eggs and sperm into the water, an event called **spawning**. This usually happens at a certain time in the moon's cycle. The **larvae** swim for a few days before settling down and secreting their own calcium-carbonate skeleton to begin a new colony.

Amazing facts

- A few corals, such as the small, solitary cup corals, can survive in the cold water off the Norwegian and Scottish coasts.
- Staghorn corals are the fastest-growing corals on a reef and would take over the reef, were it not for the fact that they are easily damaged in storms. The massive, encrusting forms such as brain corals are wave-resistant.

Jellyfish

Jellyfish are bell-shaped animals that float in the upper layer of the ocean. They get their name from the extra-thick layer of jelly between their ectoderm and endoderm.

Body features

The body of the jellyfish is like a bell with a mouth hanging down from the underside. Around the mouth are extensions called oral arms. Masses of **tentacles** hang down from the bell, each covered in thousands of sting cells. The sting cells shoot out a poisonous harpoon-like thread whenever they are triggered by touch. In many **species**, the rim of the bell contains organs that sense balance and orientation. It also contains photoreceptors that are sensitive to light, so the animal can work out which way to move towards the surface of the water.

Jellyfish swim by contracting muscle fibres in their bell. As the bell contracts, water is forced out and this pushes the jellyfish along. The bell relaxes and takes in water. When it is fully stretched, it contracts its bell again. However, this movement is weak and jellyfish cannot swim against a current. Normally they drift, carried by the ocean currents. They are often washed up on beaches after storms.

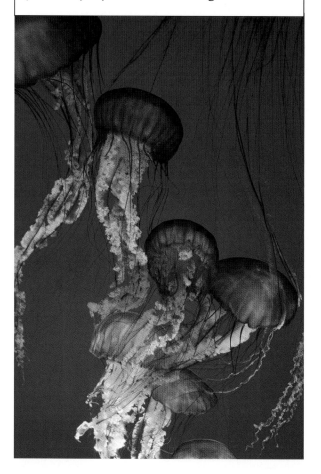

▼ Swarms of jellyfish called sea nettles occur off the coast of the eastern USA in summer. Their presence in the water prevents people from swimming.

Amazing facts

- A jellyfish's body is 96 per cent water.
- Jellyfish vary in size, with the diameter of the bell ranging from less than 2 centimetres to more than 2 metres. The largest jellyfish is *Cyanea arctica*, which has tentacles that reach lengths of 40 metres!
- Many jellyfish are bioluminescent, which means they can produce their own light. Some produce light to frighten away **predators**.

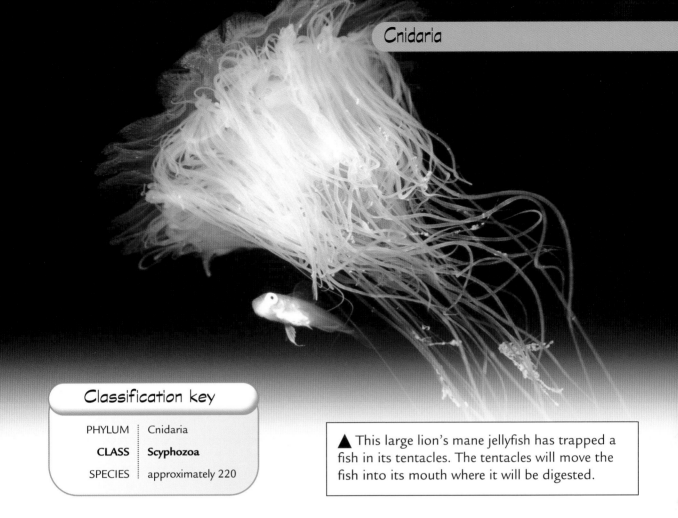

Classification key

PHYLUM	Cnidaria
CLASS	**Scyphozoa**
SPECIES	approximately 220

▲ This large lion's mane jellyfish has trapped a fish in its tentacles. The tentacles will move the fish into its mouth where it will be digested.

Feeding

Jellyfish are **carnivores** and they eat mostly **plankton** and young fish. First they stun their **prey** with their sting cells and then they use their tentacles to bring the food to their mouth. Some jellyfish swim to the surface, turn over and then float downwards, with their tentacles trailing, forming a wide net in which **crustaceans** and small fish become entangled.

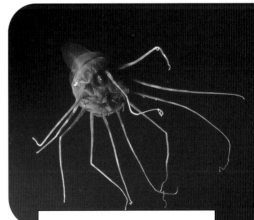

Life cycle

Most jellyfish are thought to live for about a year. Their life cycle starts with **larval** jellyfish settling on the seabed. These grow into **polyps**, which **reproduce** asexually by budding. Tiny **medusae** are pinched off the parent polyp and drift away in the water. These medusae grow into the adult jellyfish. The adults reproduce sexually by releasing **gametes** into the water. **Fertilization** takes place and the resulting larvae grow into polyps, starting the cycle again.

▲ Deep sea jellyfish have stiff tentacles. They are found at depths between 200 and 7000 metres, although at night many can be found near the surface, where they feed.

Hydrozoa

The Hydrozoa class is very varied. Some hydrozoans are small, but others are huge and they come in a range of colours and shapes. The Hydrozoa is usually divided into five orders: Trachylinida, Hydroida, Milleporina, Stylasterina and Siphonophorida.

Amazing facts

- Milleporina and Stylasterina are known as 'fire corals' because of their coral-like growth and painful sting.
- Some of the jellyfish-like medusae can rise or descend as much as 300 metres in the water in an hour.
- Hydrozoans of the genus *Hydractinia* form a dense covering over the shells occupied by hermit crabs. They are thought to defend the crab from **predators**, while benefiting from scraps of food that the crab carries around.

Hydra

One of the best known hydrozoans is *Hydra,* which belongs to the order Hydroida. These tiny freshwater animals are about 1 centimetre long and consist of a tube that ends in a ring of **tentacles** around the mouth. The colour of each **species** of *Hydra* is produced by microscopic green algae living in its cells.

▶ There are two types of polyp on this sea fir, which belongs to the genus *Obelia*. There are feeding polyps with tentacles and reproductive polyps producing medusae.

▲ The by-the-wind sailor belongs to the order Stylasterina. It is blown across the oceans as the wind catches its upright triangular float.

Classification key

PHYLUM	Cnidaria
CLASS	**Hydrozoa**
ORDERS	Trachylinida, Hydroida, Milleporina, Stylasterina and Siphonophorida
SPECIES	approximately 2700

Animals of the *Hydra* genus use a sticky disc at the end of their bodies to attach themselves to waterweed or stones. When they want to move quickly, they somersault. They bend over and attach their tentacles to the ground and then swing their base over their tentacles to land on the other side.

Colonies

The *Hydra* genus is unusual in that it lives alone. Most of the other hydrozoans form **colonies** that number thousands of **polyps**. Hydrocorals form large colonies that secrete a hard **skeleton** and resemble corals. Other hydrozoans form mats that are often mistaken for seaweed. Some of the largest hydrozoans that form colonies are confused with jellyfish.

▼ Hydrocoral is usually pink or purple and it can be found at depths of up to 20 metres.

Medusae

Just like other cnidarians, hydrozoans have a life cycle in which there are polyps and **medusae**. The medusa resembles a jellyfish. One feature that distinguishes it from the medusae of other species is the presence of a structure called a velum. This is a shelf or rim that projects inward around the edge of the bell, partially closing the opening. The hydrozoan medusae swim just like the jellyfish, by alternately contracting and relaxing the muscles in the bell. The advantage of a partially closed opening is that water can be pushed out with greater force, moving the animal by a sort of 'jet propulsion'.

The Portuguese man-of-war

The Portuguese man-of-war may look like a jellyfish, but it belongs to the class Hydrozoa. It is a gigantic **colony** of individual **polyps** floating on the ocean. Hanging below are metres of **tentacles** covered in sting cells. The man-of-war is found in warm seas around the world, especially in **tropical** and subtropical regions of the Pacific and Indian oceans, and in the northern Atlantic Gulf Stream.

▶ The blue gas-filled float of the Portuguese man-of-war lies on the surface of the water where it catches the wind. Hanging below are many long tentacles.

Classification key

PHYLUM	Cnidaria
CLASS	Hydrozoa
ORDER	Siphonophora
FAMILY	Physaliidae
GENUS	*Physalia*
SPECIES	***Physalia physalis***

Catching the wind

The man-of-war's body consists of a gas-filled float called the pneumatophore. This is translucent pink, blue, or violet. The float is as much as 30 centimetres long and rises 15 centimetres or so above the water. It acts as a sail. Hanging beneath the pneumatophore are long tentacles up to 50 metres in length. They are covered in three types of polyp – one responsible for detecting and capturing **prey**, one for digesting prey and one for producing and releasing the **gametes** that the man-of-war needs to **reproduce**. The three types of polyp are totally dependent on each other.

Feeding

The man-of-war eats anything that comes into contact with its stinging polyps, including **crustaceans** and small fish. As it drifts in the ocean, its long tentacles trail through the water. Once a prey animal has been caught, muscles in the tentacles contract and bring the prey close to the polyps that digest food.

Life cycle

The life cycle starts with the man-of-war reproducing sexually. The reproductive polyps release **gametes** into the water. **Fertilization** takes place when the gametes fuse and form a new individual. This grows into a **larva**. The larval man-of-war reproduces asexually by budding, but the buds do not separate. They remain attached, forming a colony. In time the colony develops into a full-sized man-of-war. The reproductive polyps form and **sexual reproduction** can take place again.

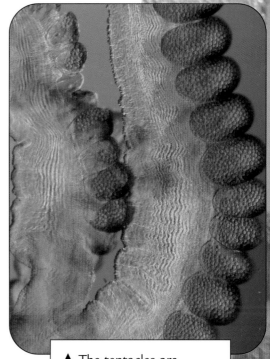

▲ The tentacles are covered in sting cells. Even a piece of tentacle broken off from the rest can give a painful sting.

Amazing facts

- The sting of the Portuguese man-of-war is very painful to humans and can have serious effects, including fever, shock and interference with heart and lung action.
- The poison released by the sting cells is about 75 per cent as powerful as cobra venom.
- Swarms, or groups, of the Portuguese man-of-war can number as many as several thousand.

Worms

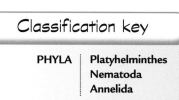
◀ Fanworms belong to the phylum Annelida because their body is made up of many segments.

The group of **invertebrates** known as worms make up three phyla: Platyhelminthes, or flatworms; Nematoda, or roundworms; and Annelida, the segmented worms. Worms are found in water, both fresh and salt, and on land, although they are restricted to damp habitats. Some worms are **parasites** that live on or in another animal, known as the **host**. The parasite feeds on the host, causing it harm.

Three cell layers

While cnidarians have two layers of cells and some of their cells are organized to form tissues, they do not have any organs. Worms, on the other hand, are more complex than the cnidarians, as they have three cell layers and distinct organs. Since they have three cell layers, they are described as **triploblastic** animals. There is an outer layer called the ectoderm, an inner layer called the endoderm and a middle layer called the mesoderm.

Classification key	
PHYLA	Platyhelminthes
	Nematoda
	Annelida

The mesoderm is very important as the cells in this layer form muscles and other structures. This allows the animal to grow larger and have a firmer body. The organs are composed of various tissues that work together to carry out a particular function, for example **reproduction**. Some of the organs work together to form a system, such as the digestive and **nervous systems**.

The most primitive of the worms are the flatworms. They have a long, flat body with no blood circulatory system. The roundworms and the segmented worms have a more complex body. The mesoderm is split to form a large, central body cavity. This cavity is filled with fluid in the segmented worms. The fluid bathes all the internal organs and gives support to the body, forming a hydroskeleton, which helps the animal to move.

Heads

While cnidarians do not have a head, worms show considerable development of one. They have a definite front end, which has sense organs and always ventures first into a new environment, with the rear end following. The sense organs allow the animal to detect any danger ahead.

▲ This is a free-living flatworm that lives in water. It belongs to the class Turbellaria in the phylum Platyhelminthes. Other classes of flatworm live as parasites on a host.

▼ Roundworms belong to the phylum Nematoda. Most live in the soil, but many are parasites, living in the bodies of other animals or on plants.

27

Flatworms

If you drop a small piece of meat into a stream, the chances are that within a few hours it will be covered in small black worms, each about one centimetre long. These are called *Planaria* and they are flatworms that live under stones in ponds and streams. *Planaria* is just one genus of flatworm that belongs to the phylum Platyhelminthes. The name comes from two words, 'platy' meaning flat and 'helminthes', referring to worms. Platyhelminthes used to be formed from three classes: Cestoda, Turbellaria and Trematoda. More recently a fourth class has been added, Monogenea.

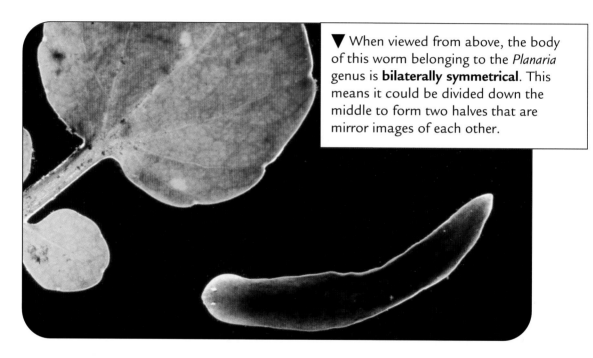

▼ When viewed from above, the body of this worm belonging to the *Planaria* genus is **bilaterally symmetrical**. This means it could be divided down the middle to form two halves that are mirror images of each other.

Body shape

Flatworms have a long, flat body. Gas exchange can take place at any point on their large surface area. The flat body means that the oxygen does not have to spread out very far to reach all the cells of the body. Some flatworms have an obvious head with eyes and other sense organs. They have a mouth that leads to a gut, but they do not have an anus at the other end of the gut. This means that the mouth is used to take in food and to expel any waste. Inside, the gut is divided into many branches so that the food reaches all parts of the body.

Classification key

PHYLUM	Platyhelminthes
CLASSES	**Cestoda, Monogenea, Trematoda and Turbellaria**
ORDERS	35
SPECIES	approximately 13,000

▶ Liver flukes are parasites that belong to the class Trematoda. They use a sucker to attach themselves to the body of their host.

Tapeworms belong to the class Cestoda. They are **parasitic** and live in the guts of **vertebrates**, including humans. Turbellaria consists mostly of free-living flatworms such as the *Planaria* genus. They are covered with tiny hairs called **cilia**. The cilia create a current that allows the animal to glide over the river or pond bottom. Trematoda and Monogenea represent the parasitic flukes. Flukes do not have cilia. They have a thick outer layer, called a **cuticle**, and **suckers**, which they use to cling on to their **host**. Some flukes cling to the outside of their host. For example, fish flukes hang on to the skin or gills of fish and feed on their blood. Other flukes invade their host's body and live in organs such as the liver.

Amazing facts

- Worms of the *Planaria* genus have amazing powers of **regeneration**. If a vertical cut is made down their head end the cells regrow to form two heads.

- Millions of people are infected by the blood fluke that causes the disease schistosomiasis. People who stand in rice paddies planting rice plants are often infected with the fluke. The parasite burrows through the skin and enters the blood system. The infected person gets gradually weaker.

▶ This marine flatworm glides over the seabed looking for food. It feeds on small **invertebrates** and dead animals.

29

The tapeworm

Tapeworms are very common **parasites** and are found in almost every **species** of **vertebrate**, including humans. Their bodies are completely **adapted** to the life of a parasite. They do not need to move around or find food, so they have no means of moving and no sense organs. They live in the intestines of their **host**, feeding on the food the host has digested. They do not even need a mouth. Instead, they absorb digested food over their huge surface area.

The tapeworm's body is divided into sections called proglottids. New proglottids form all the time from behind the head. The oldest are at the tail end of the tapeworm and they drop off when they are mature. Each proglottid has its own set of reproductive organs and by the time it drops off it is full of **fertilized** eggs. These proglottids pass out with the host's **faeces**.

Classification key

PHYLUM	Platyhelminthes
CLASS	Cestoda
GENUS	*Taenia*
SPECIES	***Taenia serialis***

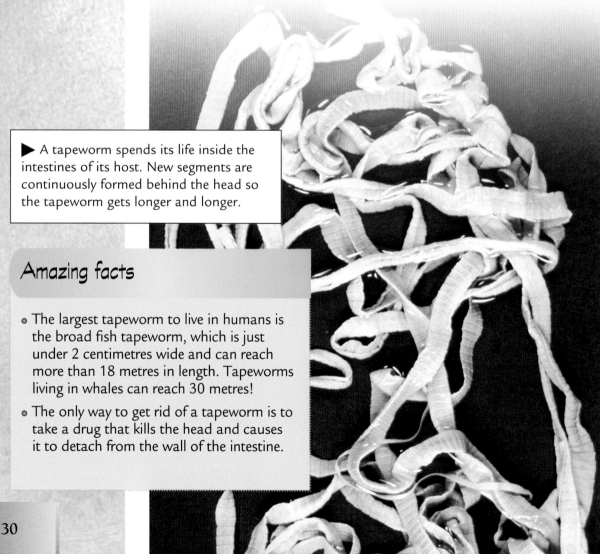

▶ A tapeworm spends its life inside the intestines of its host. New segments are continuously formed behind the head so the tapeworm gets longer and longer.

Amazing facts

- The largest tapeworm to live in humans is the broad fish tapeworm, which is just under 2 centimetres wide and can reach more than 18 metres in length. Tapeworms living in whales can reach 30 metres!
- The only way to get rid of a tapeworm is to take a drug that kills the head and causes it to detach from the wall of the intestine.

Life cycle

All tapeworms have a life cycle that involves
two hosts. Most tapeworms are species
specific – the adult will only grow in one
particular species. For example, it may
infect dogs and not cats. One type of dog
tapeworm lives in two hosts, the dog and
the rabbit. The primary, or main, host is the
dog. Eggs of the tapeworm pass out of the dog's
intestines in its faeces. Rabbits may pick up the
eggs when they feed on grass. Inside the rabbit's stomach
the hard protective coat of the egg is digested and the
embryo is released. It is armed with six sharp hooks,
which it uses to burrow through the stomach wall into the
blood stream. It is carried in the blood to the muscles,
where it settles and grows into a bladderworm.

There is no further development until the rabbit is killed and the
muscle eaten by a dog. Inside the dog, the head of the bladderworm
attaches to the wall of the intestine. Surrounded by an abundant
supply of food, the tapeworm soon grows a long body and starts to
produce eggs.

▲ Once the bladderworm
has entered the intestine of a
dog, the head of the
tapeworm is released and it
becomes attached to the
intestinal wall.

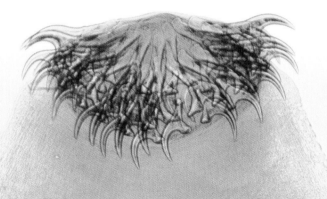

◄ The head of the dog
tapeworm bears hooks and
suckers. These are used to
attach the tapeworm firmly to
the intestinal wall. This
means the tapeworm is not
carried out of the intestine as
the food passes through.

Roundworms

Roundworms, or nematodes, are among the most abundant of all animals. They are found in almost every kind of habitat. They live in the sea, in fresh water and in soil, from the polar regions to the **tropics**. There are so many roundworms that a spadeful of soil probably contains millions of them.

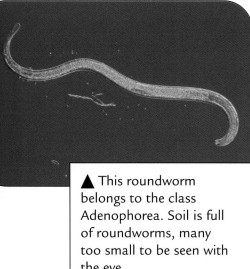

▲ This roundworm belongs to the class Adenophorea. Soil is full of roundworms, many too small to be seen with the eye.

Many species

There are two classes of roundworm, Secernentea and Adenophorea. The secernentean worms are mostly **parasites** while the adenophoreans are mostly free-living worms. Only about 15,000 **species** of roundworm have been described by scientists so far, but it has been estimated that there may be closer to 500,000 species. About 50 species have been found in humans, of which 12 are parasitic.

▼ Roundworms are found in water, too. The pointed ends of the worm can be clearly seen.

Classification key

PHYLUM	Nematoda
CLASSES	2 (Secernentea, Adenophorea)
SPECIES	15,000 described, but likely to be more than 500,000

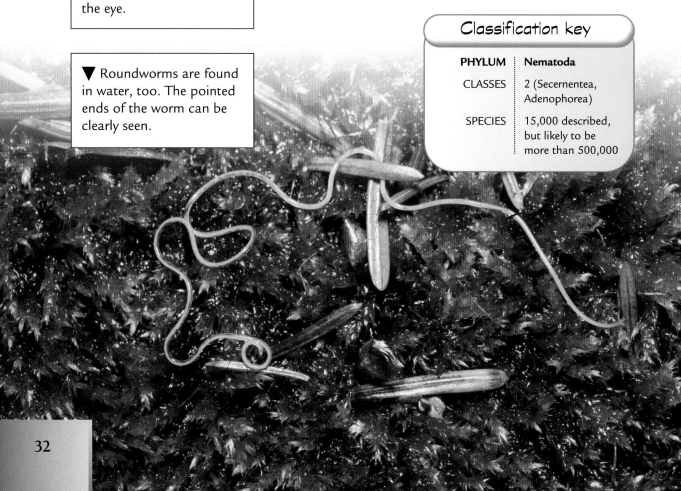

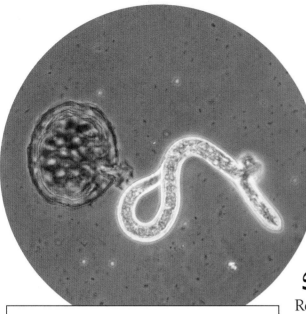

▲ This roundworm has just hatched from its egg. The egg has a tough outer wall to protect it from being digested by the **host**.

Appearance

Roundworms have a long, cylindrical body with pointed ends. The body is covered with a tough, stiff **cuticle**, which is secreted by the ectoderm. This cuticle is replaced four times between hatching and reaching full maturity.

Sideways movement

Roundworms have an unusual sideways thrashing movement. This is because they have four blocks of muscles, which run the length of their body from the head to the tail. When the muscles on one side of the body contract, the body is bent to one side. When the muscles on the other side contract, the body is bent in the opposite direction. This is a very slow and inefficient way of moving around.

Parasites

There are many parasitic species of roundworm. One that is particularly important is the roundworm *Ascaris lumbricoides*, which lives in the intestine. It is thought to infect one-sixth of the world's human population. The worm releases hundreds of thousands of eggs each day, which leave the body in the **faeces**. In places where hygiene is poor, the eggs may contaminate food or water and then pass into other humans. Once the eggs are in the stomach, the tiny worms break out and enter the blood stream. They can block small blood vessels, especially those in the lungs. This causes fluid to collect in the lungs, resulting in a serious form of pneumonia. These worms eventually return to the intestines where they develop into adult worms.

Amazing facts

- Some roundworms occur only in very precise locations. One species is found only on felt coasters placed under beer mugs in a few towns in Germany.
- One study reported around 90,000 individual roundworms in a single rotting apple.

Segmented worms

The annelids, or segmented worms, are found around the world. Marine annelids live everywhere from shallow coastal waters to the deepest ocean sediments. Some marine annelids drift and swim across the seas, **preying** on **plankton**. On land, earthworms are found in soil, while leeches live in fresh water or in damp places such as steamy rainforests.

▲ This giant earthworm, which lives in a rainforest, has come to the surface after a rain storm.

Tubular body

The body of an annelid is rather like a tube within a tube. The outer tube is the body wall made up of the ectoderm and two layers of muscles. The inner tube is the gut or endoderm. Between the two is the body cavity, or coelom, which is filled with fluid. This fluid provides a firm base for the muscle to push against as the worm moves around.

Annelids are far more complex worms than flatworms. They have a well-developed blood circulation with blood vessels and five simple hearts to pump the blood around the body. Their gut has a mouth and an anus. This means that food can be continuously taken in by the mouth, processed as it passes through the body and released as waste at the other end. They also have a simple **nervous system**. Annelids absorb oxygen from the air through their moist skin.

▶ The spaghetti worm is a marine worm. It hides its body in a tube and sends long, pasta-like **tentacles** out to bring food to its mouth.

Segments

Annelids have a body that is made up of many parts called segments. Each segment is separated from the neighbouring segments and has its own organs to carry out **respiration**, **excretion** and movement. The only parts of the body that do not follow this pattern are the head, which bears the sense organs, and the very last segment of the body.

Chaetae

A distinctive feature of annelids is their **chaetae** or bristles. Chaetae vary in shape, ranging from long thin filaments to multi-pronged hooks. The two annelid classes differ in the number and size of the chaetae. The Polychaeta, as the name suggests, have many chaetae, while the earthworms in the class Clitellata have few chaetae.

Amazing facts

- The word Annelida comes from the Latin word *anellus*, meaning 'a little ring', in reference to the ring-like segments of these worms.
- The giant earthworms of Australia can be found by the gurgling sounds they make as they tunnel underground. They are 4 metres long and have up to 500 segments.
- Small worms live for only 45–60 days, but some of the really large ones may live to more than 50 years of age.

Classification key

PHYLUM	Annelida
CLASSES	2 (Polychaeta, Clitellata)
SPECIES	approximately 12,000

◀ The fireworm has hollow, poison-filled bristles. They break off and then embed themselves in **predators**, such as fish.

Polychaetes

Polychaeta is the largest and most varied of the annelid classes and includes bristle worms, lugworms and fanworms. The Latin word *polychaetae* means 'many **chaetae**', or bristles. Some of the polychaetes are free-living, but many live in burrows or tubes.

Amazing facts

- The fireworms have chaetae made of calcium carbonate or silica, which are brittle and contain poisons. When the chaetae penetrate the skin, they break and cause a burning sensation.

- The palolo worm lives in coral **reefs**. To reproduce, it grows a tail section packed with either sperm or eggs. Five days after the first full moon in October, the tail sections of all the palolo worms break free and wiggle to the surface of the water where the released eggs are fertilized by the released sperm.

▼ The bobbit worm often lies in the sediment on the seabed. It pounces on small fish swimming above it, pulling the fish under the sediment to be eaten.

Features

One characteristic feature of the class is a structure called a **parapodium**. The word means 'side foot' and it is a flap that sticks out of the side of each segment and has chaetae growing from it. Polychaetes have well-developed heads with between two and four pairs of eyes, a number of sensory 'feelers' and a brain. Many have powerful jaws and long **tentacles** that collect food. Most have a well-developed blood circulation.

Classification key

PHYLUM	Annelida
CLASS	**Polychaeta**
ORDERS	22
SPECIES	9000

▼ This ragworm swims using its parapodia as paddles to push through the water.

▼ Most fireworms are **scavengers**. This fireworm is searching for food in the open shell of a dead clam.

Life style

Polychaetes can be divided into two types, those that are free-living and those that live **sedentary** lives. The free-living polychaetes have well-developed parapodia with chaetae, which they use to swim. The most active **species** need plenty of oxygen so some of their parapodia are modified to form gills. The free-swimming worms are usually **carnivorous** and they can chase after their **prey**, such as other worms and small **invertebrates**.

The sedentary worms spend much of their time in burrows in the mud or sand, or in tubes that they have built. Examples include lugworms, parchment worms and fanworms.

Reproduction

A few polychaetes can **reproduce** asexually by budding or dividing their bodies into separate parts. However, most polychaetes reproduce sexually. Polychaete worms are either male or female. The worms gather together and release eggs and sperm into the water at the same time. The eggs are **fertilized** and develop into free-swimming **larvae** that drift with the **plankton** before developing into adult polychaetes.

Fanworms

Fanworms are polychaetes that secrete a tube around their body. They vary in size from just a few centimetres to several metres in length. The fan of **tentacles** that emerges from the tube is often brightly coloured. Fanworms are found in coastal waters, on coral **reefs** and thousands of metres deep on the ocean floor.

Tubes

The fanworm builds a tube to protect its soft body by producing a leathery **mucus** from a collar-like structure at the base of its tentacles. Particles of sand and mud that are collected in the tentacles are incorporated into the tube. Some tubes are very long and stick out above the seabed. Others are buried in the mud or sand and are difficult to spot. These worms are very sensitive to shadows and vibrations. If they are disturbed they quickly pull back into their tube and close a 'trap door' over the top.

▲ The fanworm feeds by extending its tentacles into the water. The tentacles trap food drifting in the water.

▼ The fanworm constructs its tube from sand and mud, glued together with mucus. The tube stands above the seabed.

The worm extends a 'fan' of tentacles from the top of the tube to feed. The tentacles extract both oxygen and food from the water. Small particles of food are flicked by tiny **cilia** towards the mouth. Larger particles are passed to a storage area, where they are mixed with mucus to lengthen the tube. Living on the seabed, the worm feeds on the food that sinks down from the ocean above.

Amazing facts

- The European fanworm attaches itself to the hulls of ships and has survived the long journeys to Australia. It has become a major marine pest along the Western Australian coastline.

- Sometimes people find large numbers of empty tubes of the bamboo worm washed up on beaches after a storm. The worms have not been killed – they have retreated inside their tubes and only the empty top part has broken off.

Christmas tree worm

One of the most attractive of the fanworms is the Christmas tree worm. Christmas tree worms **spawn** in October at low tide. The eggs are **fertilized** and grow into **larvae** that settle on coral. Once settled on the coral it starts to secrete its tube.

▼ The Christmas tree worm gets its name from its brightly coloured tentacles, arranged in a spiral.

Classification key

PHYLUM	Annelida
CLASS	Polychaeta
SUB-CLASS	Sedentaria
FAMILY	**Sabellidae**
SPECIES	approximately 9000

Clitellates

The clitellates are annelids that have a swelling behind the head called a clitellum. These worms have bodies with few or no **chaetae**. The class is divided into two sub-classes, Hirudinea (leeches) and Oligochaeta (earthworms).

Earthworms

Earthworms are burrowing worms that live in soil. At night they extend the front half of their body from their burrow in search of food such as leaves and seeds. The hind end stays firmly in the burrow. Worms spend most of their time eating leaves or soil. The food passes through their gut where the valuable nutrients are digested. The rest passes out and is deposited in a pile by the entrance to their burrow. These piles are called worm casts.

Classification key

PHYLUM	Annelida
CLASS	**Clitellata**
SUB-CLASSES	2 (Oligochaeta, Hirudinea)
SPECIES	approximately 3000

Amazing facts

- It is incredibly difficult to pull an earthworm from its burrow because it pushes its chaetae into the soil that forms the burrow walls.
- Earthworms have a giant nerve fibre that runs the length of their body. This allows nerve impulses to travel quickly and is essential for the worm's escape response. If a worm is touched by a bird or other **predator**, for example, it will suddenly contract its whole body and disappear into its burrow.

▲ The front end of the earthworm is more pointed than the hind end. Here the head of an earthworm emerges from its burrow.

▼ An earthworm is pulling a leaf into its burrow. There may be between 50 and 500 earthworms in every square metre of soil. Their castings make the soil richer.

Moving

Earthworms have a simple **nervous system** that co-ordinates muscle contraction during movement. The worm uses its two sets of muscles to move. When the circular muscles contract, each segment becomes long and thin. When the muscles that stretch along the length of the worm (longitudinal muscles) contract, it becomes short and fat. First the worm extends the front of its body by contracting the circular muscles in these segments. It sticks out its chaetae to grip the soil. Then it pulls the back end of its body forwards, by contracting its longitudinal muscles. By alternating these two muscle sets, the worm can move forwards.

Reproduction

Earthworms have both male and female sex organs so they are **hermaphrodite**. However, whenever they meet another worm they will exchange sperm. During egg laying, the clitellum secretes a ring of **mucus** which glides forwards over the body of the worm. As it moves, it picks up both eggs and sperm, and **fertilization** takes place in the mucus. Then the ring slips off the worm and lies in soil. It hardens to form a cocoon in which the eggs develop and from which the young worms finally escape.

▼ This pair of earthworms are exchanging sperm. The head of one worm lies in the opposite direction to the head of the other worm.

Leeches

Leeches are found in a wide variety of habitats, especially shallow, slow-flowing streams, lakes and ponds. They are very numerous in water that is rich in nutrients, for example lakes and ponds polluted with farm waste and sewage. Leeches are also found in **tropical** rainforests. Many people think all leeches are blood suckers. Although there are many blood-sucking **species**, there are also leeches that **scavenge** on dead and decaying matter.

▲ Leeches, such as this medicinal leech, have a small sucker beside the mouth and a larger one at the rear end, which they use to attach to host animals.

▼ A tiger leech waits for a host animal to pass close by. It extends its body and will drop the instant it senses an animal passing below.

Features

Leeches have between 32 and 34 segments in their bodies, regardless of the size of the leech. Once this number is reached, they do not grow any more. In other annelids, the number of segments increases with age. Strangely, the rings on the outside of the body of the leech do not correspond to the segments inside the body. Leeches do not have any **chaetae**, so the outside of their body is smooth.

Amazing facts

- The giant Amazonian leech, *Haementeria ghiliani*, reaches just over 30 centimetres in length.

- Some leeches can survive periods of drought by burrowing into the mud at the bottom of lakes and ponds. They can tolerate the loss of 90 per cent of their body weight.

- The saliva of the medicinal leech contains substances that act as powerful antibiotics and anaesthetics (painkillers). These could be very useful in treating patients in the future.

▼ The saliva of the leech contains a substance called hirudin, which stops the host's blood from clotting while the leech is feeding.

Blood suckers

Most leeches are semi-**parasitic**, feeding on the blood of **vertebrates**. Unlike parasitic flatworms, they have to move to find a **host**, so they have sense organs and they can swim. Once a leech has found a suitable host, it attaches itself to the outside using the larger rear **sucker**. It uses small jaws around its mouth to make a small wound. The leech drops off once its gut is swollen with blood, and then it digests its huge meal. Leeches do not feed often, so they take in enough blood to last for several months.

Medicinal leeches

The medicinal leech, as its name suggests, was used in the past for medicinal purposes, mainly to remove what was thought to be 'bad blood' from diseased patients. Now the medicinal leech is making a comeback. Today it is used to relieve the build up of pressure and restore blood circulation in patients who have had severed parts of their body reattached, for example fingers and ears. The leeches can also stop scabs from forming and sealing over a wound too quickly.

Echinoderms

Echinoderms are spiny-skinned animals such as starfish, sea urchins and sea cucumbers. They are marine animals found around the world, on rocky and sandy shores, in estuaries, on coral **reefs** and on the seabed.

Spiny skeleton

The three most common characteristics of echinoderms are a **symmetrical** body that is usually divided into five parts, tube feet and a **skeleton**. The skeleton lies just underneath the skin. It is formed from plates of calcium carbonate. The plates remain separate in starfish and brittlestars, but are fitted together to form a more rigid ball shape in sea urchins. Spiny extensions and knobs stick out from the body.

▲ Echinoderms, such as this starfish, have no head or tail but they do have a mouth. The mouth of the starfish is on its lower surface.

Water vascular system

Echinoderms have an unusual system of water-filled tubes or canals that run through their body. Water is sucked into the system through a perforated plate called the madreporite that usually lies on the surface of the body. A canal leads from the madreporite to a circular canal around the mouth. Further canals lead off this circular canal down each of the arms of the animal. The canals end in rows of **tentacles** called tube feet.

▲ Sea urchins are spherical in shape. Their body is completely encased in a spiny skeleton.

Regrowing body parts

Some echinoderms have excellent powers of **regeneration**. Starfish often regrow arms bitten off by **predators** and, if disturbed, brittlestars shed an arm or part of an arm. This allows them to escape while the cast-off arm continues to wriggle, distracting the attacker. It was this behaviour that gave them the name 'brittlestar'.

However, regeneration is only possible so long as part of the arm remains attached to the central disc.

▲ Brittlestars belong to the class Ophuroidea. They have a small body with five long arms.

Five classes

The phylum Echinodermata is formed of two sub-phyla, Pelmatozoa and Eleutherozoa. Sub-phylum Pelmatozoa contains one class, Crinoidea. This is an ancient group that contains sea lilies and featherstars. Eleutherozoa is divided into four classes: Asteroidea includes starfish or seastars, Ophuroidea includes brittlestars and basket stars, Echinoidea includes sea urchins, and Holothuroidea includes sea cucumbers.

Amazing facts

- The word *echinodermata* is Greek for 'spiny skin'.
- The regeneration of an arm may take as long as a year to complete.
- The spines of many **species** of sea urchin are very thin and brittle, and sometimes are coated in a poisonous substance or have a poison gland attached.

Classification key

PHYLUM	Echinodermata
SUB-PHYLA	2 (Pelmatozoa, Eleutherozoa)
CLASSES	5 (Crinoidea, Asteroidea, Ophuroidea, Echinoidea, Holothuroidea)
SPECIES	approximately 6000

Starfish

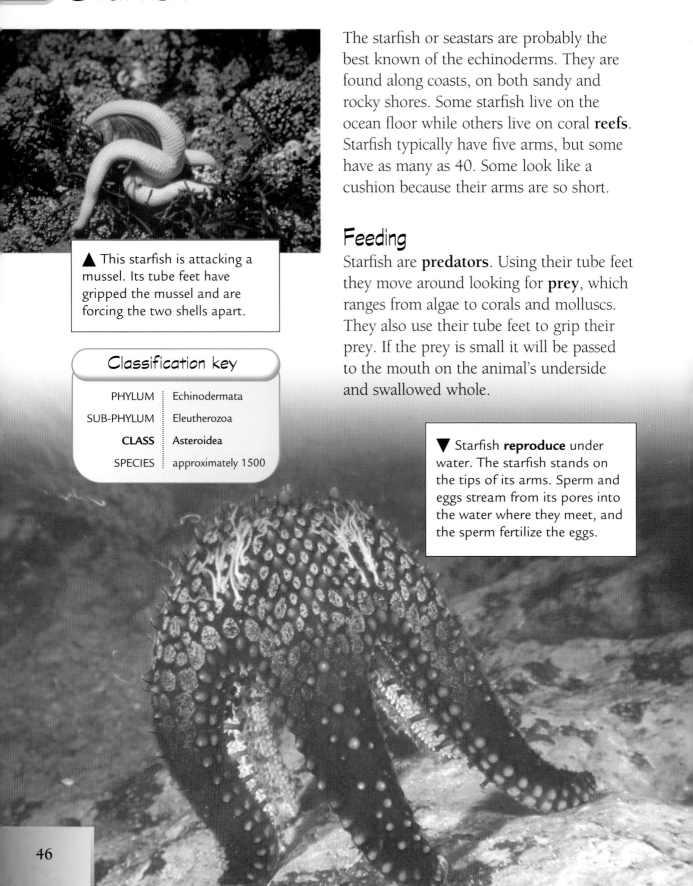

The starfish or seastars are probably the best known of the echinoderms. They are found along coasts, on both sandy and rocky shores. Some starfish live on the ocean floor while others live on coral **reefs**. Starfish typically have five arms, but some have as many as 40. Some look like a cushion because their arms are so short.

Feeding

Starfish are **predators**. Using their tube feet they move around looking for **prey**, which ranges from algae to corals and molluscs. They also use their tube feet to grip their prey. If the prey is small it will be passed to the mouth on the animal's underside and swallowed whole.

▲ This starfish is attacking a mussel. Its tube feet have gripped the mussel and are forcing the two shells apart.

Classification key

PHYLUM	Echinodermata
SUB-PHYLUM	Eleutherozoa
CLASS	Asteroidea
SPECIES	approximately 1500

▼ Starfish **reproduce** under water. The starfish stands on the tips of its arms. Sperm and eggs stream from its pores into the water where they meet, and the sperm fertilize the eggs.

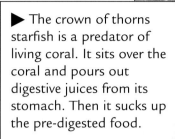

▶ The crown of thorns starfish is a predator of living coral. It sits over the coral and pours out digestive juices from its stomach. Then it sucks up the pre-digested food.

The starfish uses its tube feet to prise open the shells of bivalves, such as clams and mussels. It wraps its arms around the two shells of the bivalve and begins the slow process of forcing them apart. Once there is a tiny gap, the starfish turns out its stomach through its mouth and inserts the stomach through the narrow gap into the bivalve. The stomach secretes digestive enzymes to break down the bivalve's body into a 'soup', which is absorbed by the lining of the stomach. A starfish can take eight hours to digest a large mussel!

Amazing facts

- A single female crown of thorns starfish can produce up to 100 million eggs per year.
- A tiny crab called *Trapezia cymodoce* protects the coral *Pocillopora damicornis* from being preyed upon by the crown of thorns starfish by breaking off its spines.
- Starfish and other echinoderms have tiny pincers on the surface of their skin called pedicellaria. These pincers catch any small animal that walks over the surface of the starfish and help to keep the surface free of debris.

Reproduction

Many starfish undergo **asexual reproduction** when parts of their body break off and **regenerate**. Sometimes the leg of a starfish will simply 'walk away' from the rest of the body. **Sexual reproduction** involves the release of **gametes** into the water. In some **species**, there is a mass **spawning** when the water reaches a certain temperature. All the starfish in the area release their eggs and sperm at the same time, increasing the chances of **fertilization**.

Sea lilies and featherstars

The sea lilies and featherstars belong to the class Crinoidea, an ancient class with many **fossil** examples. Sea lilies are found in deep water while featherstars are found mostly on coral **reefs**. Featherstars with their long feathery arms are among the most beautiful of reef animals.

Sea lilies

Sea lilies can be found at depths of 100 metres or more. They are made up of three parts. The animal is attached to the seabed by its central stalk. The middle part of the individual is called the cup or calyx. Attached to the cup are five long arms. Sea lilies remain attached to the central stalk throughout their life. The stalk lifts the crown of arms above the seabed so that it is more likely to catch small animals.

Featherstars

Featherstars have five long arms and they look very similar to sea lilies. However, they break away from their stalk when they are young and become free living. Instead of stalks, featherstars have a cluster of curling root-like structures to attach themselves to coral or rock. Some featherstars can swim considerable distances.

Amazing facts

- One **extinct** crinoid, *Extracrinus subangularis,* had a stalk over 21 metres long.
- In places on the Great Barrier Reef, featherstars swarm in large numbers, covering the floor of tidal pools with great brown masses of writhing bodies.

◀ The five arms of a featherstar are divided many times and the featherstar extends its arms to feed.

▲ The arms of a featherstar look like bird feathers and gave the animal its name.

Filter feeders

Both featherstars and sea lilies are filter feeders, using their arms to catch food. Featherstars are nocturnal, only extending their arms at night to feed on **plankton**. They do not move around very much, but find a position on the reef where currents bring a constant supply of small animals. Often they are found sitting on fan corals because these corals grow in places where there is a current. Once in position, they stretch out their arms to form a fan. Each arm has a double row of tube feet, which line a sticky groove that runs down the arm to the mouth. The mouth is on top of its calyx. When a piece of food touches an arm it is grabbed by a tube foot. Then it is moved along the sticky food grooves into the mouth.

Reproduction

Sea lilies and featherstars can **regenerate** lost arms, just like starfish and brittlestars. The adult animals are of separate sexes and they undergo **sexual reproduction**. The eggs and sperm are released into the water and the **fertilized** eggs develop into free-swimming **larvae**, which settle on the seabed and develop into miniature sea lilies and featherstars.

Classification key

PHYLUM	Echinodermata
SUB-PHYLUM	Pelmatozoa
CLASS	**Crinoidea**
SPECIES	approximately 630

Sea urchins

Sea urchins look very different from starfish. They have a spherical or ball-shaped body that is covered in spines. Most sea urchins are between 6 and 12 centimetres in diameter, but some are as large as 35 centimetres in diameter. Sea urchins are found in a variety of marine habitats. Some live among the rocks of rocky shores and on coral **reefs**. Others are found buried in the sand of beaches and estuaries.

A ball of spines

Sea urchins do not have arms. They are either spherical or flattened in shape. The **skeleton** is made up of five closely fitting plates, which form a rounded shell completely enclosing the soft parts. Numerous spines stick out from the shell. The spines are joined to the skeleton by a ball-and-socket joint, rather like that of the human hip or shoulder. This means the spine can move in the joint. Sea urchins use their spines to wedge themselves in holes and crevices.

Classification key	
PHYLUM	Echinodermata
SUB-PHYLUM	Eleutherozoa
CLASS	**Echinoidea**
SPECIES	just under 1000

▶ The sea urchin moves by extending its tube feet. The tube feet grip the seabed and pull the animal forwards.

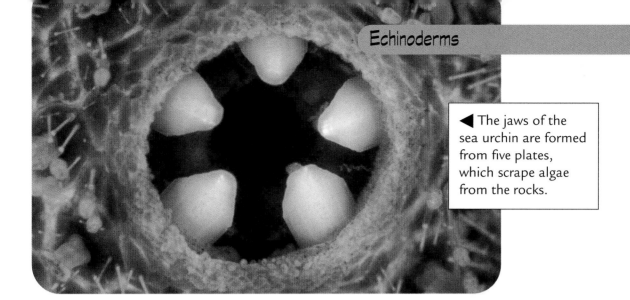

◀ The jaws of the sea urchin are formed from five plates, which scrape algae from the rocks.

Rows of tube feet

There are five rows of long tube feet, hidden amongst the spines, which the sea urchin uses to help it to move. It extends its tube feet beyond the spines. The **suckers** on the tube feet grip the surface and pull the animal along.

Feeding

Sea urchins hide in crevices during the day and emerge at night to feed. They creep slowly over rocks looking for algae and small animals. The mouth is on their underside. Surrounding the mouth are five jaw plates, which act as powerful scraping tools.

The burrowing **species** feed in a different way. They feed on particles of food that they find in the mud and sand in which they are buried. Their tube feet pass the food particles to the mouth. The sea potato has extra-long tube feet on its upper side, which it uses to dig a tunnel up to the surface in order to reach the water.

Amazing facts

- Sea urchins of the *Diadema* genus have long, thin, brittle spines that break easily. The spines are covered in a poison that causes severe irritation. People often tread on these urchins and get spines embedded in their feet.

- Despite their protective spines, sea urchins are eaten by other animals, such as the octopus and triggerfish. The triggerfish bites off the spines so that it can crack open the body of the urchin.

- Young sand dollars swallow heavy sand grains to weigh themselves down so they do not get carried away by the tides.

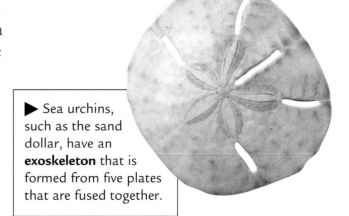

▶ Sea urchins, such as the sand dollar, have an **exoskeleton** that is formed from five plates that are fused together.

Brittlestars and sea cucumbers

Brittlestars look like slender starfish with long arms and a tiny central disc. They belong to the class Ophuroidea. The sea cucumber looks nothing like a starfish. It is a sausage-shaped animal with a leathery skin. It belongs to the class Holothuroidea.

Brittlestars

Brittlestars are found in large numbers on the seabed. They have five very long, snake-like feathery arms that they use to move over the seabed and to swim. Brittlestars do not rely on tube feet for movement and are the fastest moving of the echinoderms. Most brittlestars are **scavengers**, feeding on dead animals on the seabed. Others are filter feeders that trap drifting particles of food in **mucus** that stretches between their arms.

▲ The arms of brittlestars are edged with rows of small spines that help the animals to feed and to fend off predators.

Classification key

PHYLUM	Echinodermata
SUB-PHYLUM	Eleutherozoa
CLASS	**Ophuroidea**
SPECIES	2000

▼ The sea cucumber has a mass of tube feet around its mouth. These are covered in mucus to trap food and mud.

Sea cucumbers

Sea cucumbers live in sandy and muddy areas. Their mouths are surrounded by a mass of modified tube feet, which form feeding **tentacles**. Most sea cucumbers feed on dead plant and animal material in the sand. Sea cucumbers have an unusual method of breathing. They take in water through their anus. Once the water is inside their body, the oxygen is removed and the water is pumped out.

A small fish called the pearl fish uses the body of the sea cucumber as a hiding place during the day. When the sea cucumber breathes, its anus opens and the fish swims inside. At night the fish emerges to feed on small fishes and shrimp.

Reproduction

The sea cucumbers undergo a mass **spawning**. Many sea cucumbers gather together on the seabed and, with their heads raised like snakes, they sway in the water as eggs and sperm are released from a pore on each cucumber's head. By spawning at the same time, there is a greater chance of their eggs being **fertilized**.

Classification key

PHYLUM	Echinodermata
SUB-PHYLUM	Eleutherozoa
CLASS	**Holothuroidea**
SPECIES	1150

Amazing facts

- Some sea cucumbers release poisons. When kept in an aquarium, sea cucumbers have been known to kill all the other animals and themselves, as the poison cannot disperse.
- When attacked by a **predator**, some **species** of sea cucumbers release sticky white tubes through their anus to entangle the attacker. These tubes are part of their respiratory system. Some predators, such as small crabs, may become so trapped in the tubes that they are unable to free themselves and die.

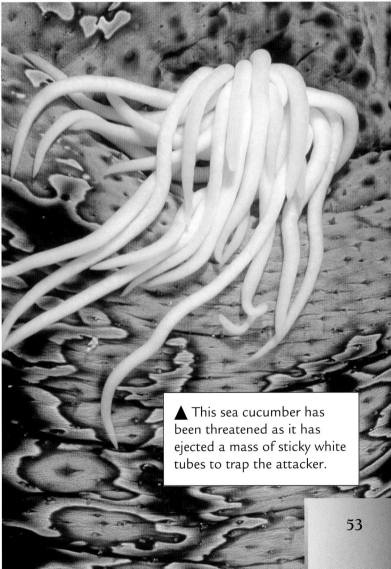

▲ This sea cucumber has been threatened as it has ejected a mass of sticky white tubes to trap the attacker.

Disappearing coral reefs

Coral **reefs** are important habitats for marine animals, as well as being made from animals themselves. They are often called the rainforests of the sea because of the great numbers of different animals and plants that live on the reefs. Unfortunately, corals are very sensitive to slight variations in water conditions and are easily damaged by pollution or environmental change.

Changing climates

An increase in the surface temperature of the water, a decrease in sea level or an increase in salinity (the amount of salt in the water) as a result of less rainfall can all affect corals. When corals are stressed by environmental changes they lose their **zooxanthellae**. This means that they cannot produce enough food. They also lose their colour and become white. This is called **bleaching**. Sometimes the corals can recover and their zooxanthellae return, but often they die. Corals under stress also suffer from more diseases. When the corals die, the rest of the habitat is affected as all the animals depend on the corals. One of the greatest threats comes from global warming. Global warming is causing the oceans to get warmer and weather patterns to change.

◄ This coral has undergone bleaching. The algae living in it have left as a result of a change in the environmental conditions, causing the coral to turn white.

Other threats

It is not only global warming that threatens coral reefs. Pollution from sewage adds nutrients to the water and this causes green algae to grow. The algae grow quickly and can completely cover a reef, preventing light from reaching the corals.

Sometimes a reef is blown up using dynamite. The broken coral can be collected and used as a building material.

There are amazing cold-water coral reefs off the coasts of Scotland, Ireland and Norway. These reefs are threatened by fishing, as nets are dragged over them to catch fish.

▲ It is very tempting for divers to touch or even break off the corals. However, the slightest touch can damage these living **organisms**.

Amazing facts

- Ten per cent of the world's reefs have already been damaged by human activity, for example by dynamiting for building materials. At current rates of destruction, this could rise to 70 per cent during the next few decades.

- Since the early 1980s humans have destroyed more than 35 million acres of coral reefs.

◀ In some places coral reefs are blown up with dynamite. The coral is sold as souvenirs and the rubble used in the building of new tourist resorts.

Protecting corals

Scientists are studying coral **reefs** to better understand them and to be able to conserve them more effectively. Many reefs are monitored using the Coral Reef Early Warning System. This system consists of buoys placed on reefs to measure air temperature, wind speed and direction, atmospheric pressure, sea temperature, salinity (levels of salt in the water) and tidal level. Every hour, this data is transmitted to scientists to tell them about conditions that may cause **bleaching** on coral reefs.

Amazing facts

- Dry Tortugas National Park in South Florida, USA, was established in 1908 as the world's first marine protected area.
- It is estimated that coral reefs may be home to more than two million **species** of plant and animal.
- Fishing from coral reefs provides food for nearly a billion people each year.

Coral reef protection

Coral reefs can be protected by making them protected areas. The many reefs of the Great Barrier Reef have been given different levels of protection. Leisure activities, such as snorkelling and diving, are allowed on some of the reefs, while fishing is allowed on others. Some of the most important reefs have the highest level of protection and cannot be visited by people at all.

▼ Scientists have found that shipwrecks are quickly **colonized** by corals and a new reef is established.

Less silt

Mangrove swamps are smelly, muddy habitats found along low-lying **tropical** coasts. The mass of tangled mangrove roots traps **silt** and prevents it reaching coral reefs. However, many mangrove swamps have been cleared to make space for new tourist resorts and marinas. In many parts of the world, these swamps are now being replanted and hopefully this will mean that more coral reefs are protected from damaging silt.

▲ Artificial reefs can be formed by sinking old trucks and army equipment in areas of ocean where the conditions are right for corals.

Looking after the reef

Local communities around the world are realizing that their coral reefs are important. For many people living on small tropical islands, such as the Maldives, fish is their main source of protein. Coral reefs are home to many fish. By protecting their coral reefs the islanders will have more fish for the future. Coral reefs are natural barriers that protect islands and coasts from storms. If the reef is destroyed, the protection is lost. Also, a healthy coral reef may help the local community earn money by attracting tourists.

► Coral reefs may contain many species of coral and support thousands of other species, making them one of the most diverse habitats on Earth.

Classification

Scientists have found and classified about 2 million different types of animals. With so many **species** it is important that they are classified into groups. The groups show how living **organisms** are related by **evolution** and where they belong in the natural world. A scientist identifies an animal by looking at its features, for example, by counting the number of legs or teeth it has. Animals that share the same **characteristics** belong to the same species. Species with similar characteristics are placed in the same genus. The genera (singular: genus) are grouped together in families, families are grouped into orders and orders are grouped into classes. Classes are grouped together in phyla (singular: phylum) and finally, phyla are grouped into kingdoms. Kingdoms are the largest groups and are at the highest level. There are five kingdoms: monerans (bacteria), protists (single-celled organisms), fungi, plants and animals.

Naming an animal

Each species has a unique scientific name, usually known as its Latin name, consisting of two words. The first word is the name of the genus to which the organism belongs and the second is the name of its species. For example, the Latin name of the common earthworm is *Lumbricus terrestris* and that of the red marsh worm is *Lumbricus rubellus*. This tells us that these animals are grouped in the same genus but are different species. Latin names are used to avoid confusion. For example, in the UK, echinoderms belonging to the class Asteroidea are usually called starfish but in other parts of the world they are called seastars. Sometimes there are very small differences between individuals that belong to the same species so there is an extra division called a sub-species. To show that an animal belongs to a sub-species, another name is added to the end of the Latin name.

◀ The starfish is classified as an echinoderm because it has a spiny skin and tube feet.

This table shows how a common starfish is classified.

Classification	Example: common starfish	Features
Kingdom	Animalia	Starfish belong to the kingdom Animalia because starfish have many cells, need to eat food, and are formed from a **fertilized** egg.
Phylum	Echinodermata	An animal from the phylum Echinodermata has a spiny skin and a body based on five parts, with tube feet.
Class	Asteroidea	Members of the Asteroidea have a circular body with five or more arms. The madreporite is found on the upper surface.
Order	Forcipulatida	These members have a **sucker** at the end of each tube foot and tiny pincers.
Family	Asteriidae	Members of this family all possess four rows of tube feet.
Genus	*Asterias*	A genus is a group of species that are more closely related to one another than to any other species in the family. *Asterias* refers to the genus.
Species	*rubens*	A species is a grouping of individuals that **interbreed** successfully. The species name of the common starfish is *Asterias rubens*.

Invertebrate evolution

Life first appeared on Earth about 3.8 billion years ago. These were the bacteria and other single-celled **organisms**. Some of these single-celled organisms **evolved** into simple animals. The next major step forward came when cells grouped together to form an animal with many cells. This animal was probably a sponge and it happened about 1 billion years ago.

▲ This is the fossil of a sea urchin. Sea urchins, starfish and sea cucumbers appeared about 250 to 200 million years ago. Sea lilies evolved earlier, during the Cambrian Period.

Most of our knowledge of the past is based on **fossils**, the hard remains of animals that are preserved in rocks. Unfortunately, the soft-bodied cnidarians and flatworms do not leave fossils. However, some scientists have found flower-like patterns on the surface of rocks, which are believed to be the marks left by jellyfish washed up on a beach. These marks date back 650 million years.

One of the most important periods in the history of the natural world is the Cambrian Period, about 540 million years ago, when life was evolving at a very fast rate. Before this time there were just sponges, cnidarians and flatworms. By the end of the Cambrian Period all the main groups of animals had appeared. One such group was the annelid worms. These burrowing worms helped to break down dead and decaying material and this process released carbon dioxide gas into the atmosphere. This gas was in short supply at the time and the plants needed it to carry out **photosynthesis**. The arrival of the annelids meant there was more carbon dioxide for the plants.

◄ Corals leave behind a limestone **skeleton**. They can be traced back to 600 million years ago.

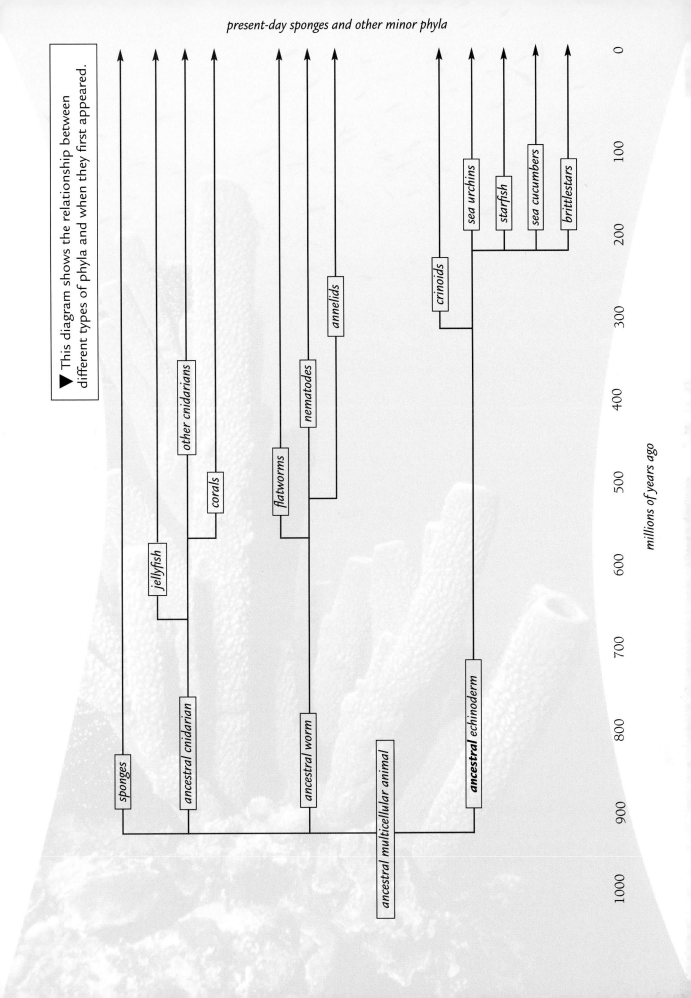

present-day sponges and other minor phyla

▶ This diagram shows the relationship between different types of phyla and when they first appeared.

sponges

jellyfish

other cnidarians

corals

ancestral cnidarian

flatworms

nematodes

annelids

ancestral worm

crinoids

sea urchins

starfish

sea cucumbers

brittlestars

ancestral echinoderm

ancestral multicellular animal

millions of years ago

0   100   200   300   400   500   600   700   800   900   1000

Glossary

adapted changed in order to cope with the environment

anemone type of marine cnidarian with a ring of tentacles around its mouth, belonging to the class Anthozoa

asexual reproduction reproduction in which one organism produces offspring that are genetically identical to the parent

bilateral on two sides

bleaching the turning white of corals following the loss of their zooxanthellae

carnivore meat-eater

chaetae tiny bristles

characteristic feature or quality of an animal, for example having tentacles or bristles

cilia tiny hairs that beat or move

colony group of individuals living as one

crustacean arthropod that has antennae, eyes on stalks and a shield-like covering over the head and thorax, for example a crab

cuticle protective outer covering found on some invertebrate animals, such as tapeworms

diploblastic having two layers of cells, called the ectoderm and endoderm

evolution slow process of change in living organisms so they can adapt to their environment

evolve to change very slowly over a long period of time

excretion removal of waste products from the body

exoskeleton skeleton made of a tough material on the outside of an animal's body

extinct no longer in existence, to have permanently disappeared

faeces waste produced by the body

fertilize to create a cell capable of becoming a new individual through the fusing of male and female sex cells (sperm and eggs)

flagellum (plural: **flagella**) long hair or thread-like structure that is attached to a cell

fossil preserved remains of an organism

gametes sex cells, such as eggs and sperm

hermaphrodite having both male and female reproductive organs

host organism on which a parasite lives and feeds

interbreed mate with another animal of the same species

intertidal zone area of shore between the lowest low tide and the highest high tide

invertebrate animal without a backbone

larva young animal that looks different from the adult and which changes appearance as it develops

medusa (plural: **medusae**) free-swimming stage in the life cycle of a cnidarian. It looks like a jellyfish.

mucus slimy substance produced by an animal's body

nervous system network of the nerve cells that carries nerve impulses between parts of the body, which allows an organism to co-ordinate its responses

organism any living thing

osculum (plural: **oscula**) name given to the large pore of a sponge, through which water leaves a sponge

parapodium (plural: **parapodia**) flap that sticks out from the side of a segment of a polychaete worm, often bearing chaetae

parasite organism, such as a tapeworm, that lives on or in another organism (called the host) and causes that organism harm

photosynthesis process by which plants make their own food using light from the Sun, carbon dioxide and water

plankton small plants and animals that drift in great numbers in the upper levels of fresh or salt water

polyp sedentary stage in the life cycle of a cnidarian

predator animal that hunts another animal

prey animal that is hunted by another animal; to hunt another animal

radial symmetry able to be divided into many equal parts arranged around a central axis

reef colony (large group) of hard corals

regeneration regrowth

reproduce to produce new organisms that are like the parent

respiration process that takes place in cells to release energy from food substances, using oxygen and releasing carbon dioxide

scavenger animal that feeds on the dead bodies of other animals

sedentary remaining in one place, hardly moving

sessile attached to the seabed and unable to move from one place to another

sexual reproduction reproduction involving the production of gametes (eggs and sperm) by two parents and the fusion of an egg and sperm to form a new individual

silt small pieces of soil, rock and other debris carried in water

skeleton framework of an animal that supports its body

spawn release eggs

species group of individuals that share many characteristics and can produce offspring

spicule small, sharp, pointed structure found in sponges and soft corals

sucker cup-shaped structure that sticks to a rock, or even another animal, using suction

symmetrical able to be divided into parts of equal shape and size

tentacles parts of the body that are long and trailing, as in jellyfish, or can be extended, as in anemones, in order to catch prey

territory area in which an animal or group of animals live

triploblastic having three cell layers, an ectoderm, mesoderm and endoderm

tropical relating to the hot regions of the world that lie either side of the equator

tropics hot, often wet, region of the world between the tropic of Cancer and the tropic of Capricorn

vertebrate animal that has a backbone

zooxanthellae algae that live in corals, providing them with food

Further information

BOOKS TO READ

Du Temple, Lesley A, *Coral Reefs* (Lucent Books, 2000)

Morgan, Sally, *Worms* (Chrysalis Children's Books, 2002)

Sheppard, Charles, *Coral Reefs: Ecology, Threats and Conservation* (Voyager Press, 2002)

Stephens, Jack, *Living Mirrors: A Coral Reef Adventure* (Umbrage Editions, 2003)

WEBSITES

http://www.mcsuk.org/index.htm
Website of the Marine Conservation Society, a UK charity dedicated to the protection of the marine environment. The site provides information on many marine animals, both invertebrate and vertebrate, as well as ways in which people can help to conserve marine environments such as coral reefs.

http://www.reef.edu.au
An Australian website operated by the Reef Education Network, looking at all aspects of coral reefs, as well as the conservation and research that is being undertaken.

www.coralreefalliance.org
The website of the Coral Reef Alliance, which promotes coral reef conservation around the world by working with the dive industry, governments, local communities and other organizations to protect and manage coral reefs, and to raise funds for conservation efforts.

http://www.seaworld.org
A website run by the Seaworld adventure parks organization of the USA, which covers many marine species and has a large section devoted to corals.

Index